THE
SMALLEST
TALK

THE
SMAL

LEST
TALK

one-line poems

MICHAEL McFEE

BULL CITY PRESS POETRY SERIES
2007

Grateful acknowledgment is given to the periodicals
in which the following poems first appeared:
"Behind the Waterfall," "Dermatographia," and
"Dead Party" in *Blink*; "The Arcade of Middle Age"
and "Sharing Chapstick" in *Inch*.

Cover photograph by Stewart Lestrade

Book design by Bull City Design
http://design.bullcitypress.com

Typeset in Georgia and Century Gothic.
ISBN-13: 978-1-4243-1797-5
ISBN-10: 1-4243-1797-5

BULL CITY PRESS
"Hit Bull, Win Steak"
1217 Odyssey Dr.
Durham, NC 27713
http://bullcitypress.com

for the Lindanians

&

in memory of
An Oar in the Old Water

CONTENTS

I.

BEHIND THE WATERFALL

Rapunzel kept letting down her high lonesome hair

EMBOUCHURE

We'd improvise kisses till our mouths were numb

FINALLY

Wearing nothing but my high-school ring

BREAKING THE COMMANDMENTS

I lowered my eyes and worshiped her golden calves

DERMATOGRAPHIA

Look how her nails spoke in tongues all over my back

II.

A SHEET OF PAPER

Blank mirror I've broken a million times

BEER

Doer's drunken cousin, draining another pitcher

PORK SKINS

"This is like chewing" — she coughed — "on fried fiberglass."

APPALACHIA

Blue echoes in my speech like hazy ridges

INCLUDING WORDS

What comes out of the body is warm, and mostly waste

III.

DRY DREAMS

Mais où sont les émissions d'antan?

THE ARCADE OF MIDDLE AGE

Who put all these funny mirrors in the bedroom?

SECOND TEENHOOD

How badly he still desires to be desired

SHARING CHAPSTICK

The closest his lips may come to touching hers

IMPOTENCE

Sorry, but this line just won't quite

IV.

DEAD PARTY

Silence is the smallest talk

MOTHER'S DAY

Cold bloom drained of blood, pinned over a coldness

BEFORE THE BULLDOZERS

Today the meadow exhaled its last purple words

X

Tilted roadside cross, its faded flowers mark the spot

CREMATORIUM

Kiln that unadams the body's unglazed clay

ABOUT THE AUTHOR

MICHAEL McFEE was born in Asheville, North Carolina, and now lives in Durham. The author of ten books of poetry and essays, he teaches at the University of North Carolina, Chapel Hill.